SELF PUBLISHING:
IT AIN'T
ROCKET SCIENCE

A Practical Guide to Writing, Publishing, and Promoting a Book

Richard L. Wren
and
Loyd Auerbach

Poor Richard Publishers
Lafayette, CA

Dynamite in a small book. Ideas galore. Examples replete. Ultimate simplicity. Every mailing address, every phone number, every e-mail address you might need to get your novel successfully written, edited and published for the least amount of dollars.

Books by Richard L. Wren
Casey's Slip
Joshua's Revenge
Justice for Joshua
Murder Made Legal (2016)

Books by Loyd Auerbach
ESP, Hauntings and Poltergeists: A Parapsychologist's Handbook
Psychic Dreaming: A Parapsychologist's Handbook
Reincarnation, Channeling and Possession
Mind Over Matter
Ghost Hunting: How to Investigate the Paranormal
Hauntings & Poltergeists: A Ghost Hunter's Guide
A Paranormal Casebook: Ghost Hunting in the New Millennium

By Loyd Auerbach & Annette Martin
The Ghost Detectives' Guide to Haunted San Francisco

By Edwin C. May, Victor Rubel, & Loyd Auerbach
ESP WARS: EAST AND WEST

TABLE OF CONTENTS

INTRODUCTION: RICHARD L. WREN:

My first book, CASEY'S SLIP, was written, self-edited and self-published just the way I've outlined herein and was chosen as one of the top 2 finalists in the nationwide Indie Excellence Book Awards of 2014 in the Action/Adventure category.

CAVEATS: In no way do I mean to disparage professional editors. My 3rd and 4th books have been edited professionally and much improved.

HOWEVER: I could not afford professional editing for my first and second books and was force to self-write, self-edit and self-publish with the aid of CreateSpace. It is for authors in that predicament that these pages are dedicated.

CREDIBILITY: Let me explain. I spent almost 5 years writing and re-writing, editing and re-editing, publishing and re-publishing CASEY'S SLIP. It was the 3rd edition, published in 2011 that won the national commendation in the aforementioned awards competition. Along the line I learned a lot, that's what's in this treatise. I sincerely believe this booklet will make it easier for you to become a published author.

Why is this book different than any other? Look on page 41.

EVERY mailing address, e-mail address, website, phone number you will ever need to write, edit and publish your book is there, painfully acquired by me over several years.

Having been a slow learner on my first book, I decided there must be an easier, faster, and better way to write, edit, and proof-read my 2nd book, all by myself. I found nothing in conventional "How To" books except offers from people trying to take more money from me. I needed to made effective shortcuts. A way to bypass the time consuming side issues that stymie so many authors. Something effective, fast, accurate, and above all, cheap!! After all, I was then 85, I didn't have all the time in the world to get where I wanted to get.

THERE HAD TO BE A BETTER WAY—AND THERE WAS!!

I created it, I followed it, and in 5 months my 2nd book was completed.

I decided that if my idea made it easier, faster and cheaper for me to write and publish a book, why not others? Thus was born my booklet. My 6 step plan is for the non-professional writer. For the average person that has a book inside himself or herself, but is overwhelmed by the enormity of "WRITING A BOOK or PUBLISHING A BOOK or EDITING A BOOK or PROOF-READING a BOOK. My booklet will help you become **UNDERWHELMED** by those problems.

Read my treatise. It's short, dynamic, succinct, fact filled, complete in one little book and cheap. About as expensive as a ream of paper. It will get you off your duff and into your novel before you know it. It will eliminate your fear of writing and publishing. It will help you stop procrastinating. It will help you become the published author you've always suspected you could be. It worked for me and it will work for you.

JUST WRITE THE DAMN THING!

INTRODUCTION: LOYD AUERBACH

I've been teaching some form of a "Publishing and Media" course at John F. Kennedy University (these days in Pleasant Hill, CA) since the very late 1980s. At the time, the graduate school asked me to put together a practical class on getting published and promoting oneself and one's practice/business/self to the media (practical skills for graduates of the university). Even at that time, I'd had some success with my first book, working with a literary agent who then sold another, and with lots of media coverage (TV, radio and print – the Internet was still not quite there).

While the publishing piece of the course was focused mainly on nonfiction, the basics of finding and working with a regular publisher (including their editorial staff) were applicable to all book projects, and I even covered magazine articles and short stories. The media part of the class focused on getting coverage (including creating a press kit) and being good interviewee. I used various books for required reading over the years for both segments of the course. Naturally, as self-publishing became easier, especially with the advent of print-on-demand publishing, I included that in the course, and more recently also began including a nice segment on using social media for promotion.

Back in the 80s, I'd written a piece on working with the media for a Bay Area writers' group magazine (a large one, called the Writers' Connection, since disappeared). I expanded that from time to time and included it in the course reader for the JFKU class. But I'd wanted something really simple for the publishing piece as well.

I met Richard Wren a few years ago, when he first wanted a brush up on his public speaking skills (something I've also taught for years, and these days I work as a public speaking and media skills coach). Once past the public speaking issues, he asked about coaching him on book promotions. As a new author of mysteries (and a unique one, having started his writing career in his 80s), he wanted help navigating the current methods and practices for promotion.

Besides his first novel, *Casey's Slip*, he also had this nifty little booklet of practical advice for folks who wanted to get past any writer's block and get quickly and easily published. The booklet was based on what he'd learned researching the publishing (traditional and self) process on his own for a couple of years, culminating in his decision to use CreateSpace for print-on-demand for that first novel, and then for the booklet.

I quickly saw the applicability of Richard's booklet to my class, and immediate adopted it as one of the required texts. For your information, it was entitled *A Practical Guide to Writing and Publishing a Novel: the Keep It Simple and Successful (K.I.S.S.) Way*.

Recently, Richard was going through a review of the booklet and we discussed not only updating it, but including some commentary for nonfiction books in his section, and including my piece on promotion as a second part of the book. The result is what you hold in your hands. My contribution includes that brief commentary on nonfiction, spaced throughout Richard's section of the book. The second half of the book is directed at promotion, of your book(s), your expertise, and yourself as either an author or expert (or both).

This little book (it's more than a booklet now) is simple. There are many more books out there that have lots more information in them, and I'd never tell you to avoid them. But this little book has distilled down a lot of what's in those other sources, based on actual practical experience. It has simple success tips in it, but all of it (especially the promotion part) requires some work on your part, just as the writing requires some work.

In essence, this book – and reviewing sources referenced in the book – is pretty much all you need besides your own time, creativity, and energy. There's certainly more to learn, especially if you want to go the traditional publishing route. But this is a great start for both new and seasoned authors who want to go the print-on-demand route, and preps you for what needs to come with respect to promoting your books, your work and yourself.

PART ONE:

Writing and Publishing a Novel

By

Richard L. Wren

(with some additional comments on nonfiction by Loyd Auerbach)

SECTION ONE: WRITING THE BOOK

STEP 1: FICTION

BUY A STENOGRAPHER'S NOTEBOOK

Sounds silly, but it works really well for me, and THIS STEP IS VERY IMPORTANT, in order to *be your own editor and save a lot of money, time and agony.* This does not mean one should avoid professional editors. This step will help you keep track of your characters and story as you write.

This is the first step in that direction. It's important to recognize what editors do for your book. They are not usually proof-readers. They make sure your book is cohesive. They will try to clean up your mess. They will try to make your book readable and marketable. If you intend to edit your own book or are forced to because of cost, you must take this step.

PROBLEM: What happens if your hero is a red-head, named George in the first chapter and somehow or another becomes a blonde named Ralph in the 4th chapter. Or another character becomes 6 feet tall in one section when he was only 5'5" earlier. How do you prevent those things from happening in the first place? How do you correct it? How do you find and correct errors and mistakes that spell-check won't find? In other words, how do you edit your own book?

FIRST, Rush to the corner drug store or dollar store and buy a stenographer's notebook. In that notebook you faithfully enter short notes about each character, *every **name** highlighted,* his or her characteristics and description, along with the page number and anything else you think important. Do this at the end of each writing session. *Do not rely on your memory.* (You'll thank me later)

Every time you come up with a new character, take the time to fully describe the character in your steno book or other note-keeping device.

THIS IS THE FIRST STEP TOWARD CONTENT EDITING YOUR OWN BOOK. It will help you avoid repetition, find and correct mistakes and make changes in the chronological development of your book. Things an editor might do for you.

A RARE SECOND CHANCE. I'd bet almost anything that you've been the situation where after an argument or making a point, you've wished that you had said THIS instead of THAT, or phrased it a different way, or made a different point than the way you did. That will happen over and over as you write. You will wake up in the middle of the night with the perfect phrase for something that you wrote two weeks ago. How do you find that spot and insert the new and perfect wording? This may be the only chance you'll ever get to correct past statements, effectively. ONLY if you can find that elusive paragraph. The notebook will make that easy. DO IT!!!

IMPORTANT NOTE.

Store the up to date copy of your work every day on a thumb drive and do it religiously. You don't want to lose several months work because of a computer glitch. (Loyd adds: "Be careful not to lose that thumb drive.")

SUMMARY

Always keep a running log of what's happening in your book. Keep a running log of the characters and their descriptions every time you set pen to paper or finger to computer. Be sure and mark down the page number relating to each entry. Write down the word count and the date also. Inevitably, as your story becomes longer and longer and more and more complex with people and situations, you will make mistakes. The log helps you avoid them. One famous author said "fiction is just a collection of lies." If that's true and it's also true that one lie begets another in order to support the first, you better keep a log.

A NOTE ABOUT NON-FICTION

Unless you're writing about your life, or telling the true story of some real events with real people, keeping track of plot, story and characters does not apply to non-fiction books.

Many writers intending to self-publish go through the exercise of writing a full blown book proposal, including not only detailed outline notes, but also an assessment of the potential readership, marketing plans, and an understanding of similar books in the marketplace.

However, be prepared to go back over what you've written to make sure you are not being repetitious or leaving things out. Using the book proposal's chapter/section outlines as checklists will help with that, or you can use Richard's steno notebook concept to track facts/anecdotes/examples/etc. as you write them.

Check the resources at the end of this book for a couple of suggested titles to help you with that, as well as a brief outline of a typical book proposal.

JUST WRITE THE DAMN THING

STEP 2

GETTING STARTED

Eliminate "I can't get started" from your thinking. It's the single most often stated complaint I hear.

The best way to write a novel is to NOT write a novel.
- Do *not* sit down at your computer and write an (ugh!) novel. (Tell a story)
- If you are *not* going to write a novel, what *are* you going to do? (Tell a story)
- Do *not* start by writing "Chapter One." It's limiting. It can promote mental blockage. (Tell a story)
- Do *not* worry about spelling, punctuation, and grammar at this point. (Tell a story)

*YOU **ARE** GOING TO TELL A STORY TO SOME OF YOUR FRIENDS IN A QUIET SETTING!!*

Loyd added "Many years ago, the fantasy author L. Sprague de Camp said something exceptional to me: when you write, tell the story or talk about the subject matter as if you had a friend sitting across from you. My first editor at Warner Books told me the same thing."

You're not teaching an English class. Your grammar, spelling, commas, quotation marks, parentheses, spacing, asterisks, exclamation points, etc. will not be judged, not yet.

"It don't make no difference no-how, at least not at this stage." All you are doing is telling a story to your friends. Talk to them as if they were in the same room with you. They don't need punctuation. You do that with your voice and inflection.

Relax, you're among friends. Put periods wherever you think they should go, do the same with commas, apostrophe etc., but don't sweat them. Write as effortlessly and smoothly as you can. Make mistakes, use bad English, mix up the dates, confuse the flow, it doesn't matter.

Just keep plowing on. All will be forgiven later. Your friends don't care. They'll bridge the gaps. Occasionally you can ask them if the story you're telling makes sense to them. (You can do the same with the written version.) Let spell check do some of the work for you, but don't rely on it. There many things it can't do, or will do wrong.

YOUR GENIUS RESIDES IN YOUR STORY TELLING, NOT IN YOUR PUNCTUATION.

Picture this. You're at a friend's house with a gathering of other old friends. Suddenly your host interrupts the festivities turns to you and says, "Charlie, I heard that your trip to the Amazon last year was a real adventure, something about headhunters and getting lost? Why don't you tell us about it?"

Do you start by saying, "CHAPTER ONE"? Of course not. It would sound silly. It would make the story-telling more laborious, less spontaneous and less interesting. It would interrupt the flow of the story and be very difficult. It would inhibit your ability to tell the story. If you type CHAPTER ONE onto your blank page, you'll probably stare at it for hours trying to get past it.

Write exactly what you might say to your friends conversationally. Lots of people would start talking by saying, "well, this's what we did............" SO, start your novel the same way. Remember, you're talking to friends, not writing a **NOVEL.** Maybe like this??

"Geez guys that was a long time ago. Lotsa' water passed under the bridge since then. Let's see. I think the whole trip was Linda's idea. She always wanted to go to Africa but we settled for the Amazon 'cause it's a shorter trip."

Type something like that AAAAND, you're off and running. Try it. Go ahead, make mistakes. Don't worry about typos, if you can't remember a name or a date just slip in a bunch of bright red XXXXX'S (or yellow highlighting, or both) and keep going. You can look them up later. No one's looking over your shoulder.

Here's something else to keep in mind. You will NOT finish your book in 3 weeks or 3 months. More likely a year, or 2. Or even 3? So what's your hurry?

Plenty of time for perfection later, much later.

QUICK NOTE ON CHARACTERS

Most readers, purchasers, critics, reviewers, agents etc. are looking for books with well-developed characters as well as a well-developed story. If you're having trouble developing in-depth characters or aren't sure, here are a couple of ideas to help you get started.

A Character development list can be found at **http://niemanstoryboard.org/stories/building-character-a-checklist/** . The list is a tool only. It gives you a check off list about characteristics of your book characters you might develop. Probably more ideas than you will want to use. Ideas like habits, peculiarities, idiosyncrasies as well as height, weight etc. Can be used to develop depth and believability.

Use TV or movie actors' pictures and bios for inspiration (or perspiration). On your computer ask for a list of actor pics that fit your hero. For example I used "male stars under age 35" for the role model of a new character. I found a picture that resembled the picture I had in my mind and printed it along with his bio. I had his photo, I knew the color of his eyes, the set of his hair, the wrinkles in his face, even what his teeth looked like when he smiled. I had his height, weight, birthdate, birthplace which I did not use. I created those statistics for my character myself. The picture is just a general reminder for me. I actually used many of them as a continuing source for in depth descriptions of my character. Easy and interesting. Nobody but you knows who you used (just be sure not to use their names).

A NOTE ABOUT NON-FICTION

While you may not be telling a story per se when writing non-fiction, you are still relating information to you reader. So always keep the ideal reader in mind when you're writing, and converse with that imaginary reader across the table or desk from you. Can you talk with them about your topic without boring them? Can you fully inform them? Educate them? Even entertain them a little?

Worst Case Scenario

You *still* can't put ideas to computer to paper. Even imagining yourself at a friend's house telling your story to a group of close friends is beyond comprehension.

HERE'S AN IDEA: Get a voice recorder. "Hire" some personal friends to help you. Sit down with them and tell them about your story and encourage them to ask questions of you about the durned thing. Answer their questions. Let one of them record the mess.

USE IT TO GET STARTED.

JUST WRITE THE DAMN THING !!

STEP 3

DON'T SWEAT THE OPENING PARAGRAPH

How do you get started? How do you create a slam bang first paragraph that will immediately hook your prospective reader? How do you find those magical first words that will set the tone for the whole book? Answer? **YOU DON'T.** What you **DO** is as follows. Sit down at your computer, turn on spell-check, and start typing. You might pretend you're talking to your host and say something like "If you really want to hear the story, here it is."

Or, you could say, "It was a dark and stormy night."

Or, "I never thought I'd live through it, but..."

Or, "Here's a story for you."

Or maybe, "once upon a time."

Or perhaps, "a funny/strange thing happened on the way here today."

OR --make it easy on yourself. Don't go for perfection, go for TRITE! Write the most mundane, foolish beginning you can imagine.

JUST DO SOMETHING, TAKE THE FIRST STEP.

The point is, it doesn't matter how you start. Open the door. Twist off the lid. Start pouring. You have a story! Tell it. Pretend you're talking to your brother or your best friend. You can search for that magical opening later. Every fiction author I've ever spoken to said they had no idea how their story was going to progress, let alone end, when they began the story.

Somewhere in your writing you'll find that elusive beginning. Maybe, eventually, the third chapter will become the first chapter. The first throwaway sentence, whatever it may be, is the most important in getting started. It opens the flood gates. It can be trite, it can be meaningless, doesn't matter. Dive in!!! In my first book, what I had intended to be the first chapter, eventually became the 4th chapter, and the original 1st chapter became a flash-back.

TRY THIS

<u>ONE</u>: If you try starting your book with a *favorable setting*, you won't have to worry about details, they'll come naturally to you. Set your opening scene someplace you're very familiar with. Your living room, a favorite restaurant, your home town, doesn't matter. Just be so familiar with the setting that you can picture it as if you were there. Have a couple of drinks, really relax. In your mind, picture every last detail of the setting you can dredge up.

For example, let's take your living room. The sunlight streaming through a window, the dust on the table, the neglected broom standing in the corner. What time of day is it? Can you hear sounds from outside? Is the morning newspaper folded on the table?

Focus your internal eye on the entire room, inch by inch. Who else is in the room? What are they doing? Something mundane? Picking their nose? What's the atmosphere? Calm? Tense? In your writing, reflect what YOU see and feel.

<u>TWO:</u> Put your character in that room. Let him glance around the room and notice those things. Establish who and where he is. You are him or her. What do you see? Do you pick up the paper? Is it open to the cross-word puzzle? Is the leather chair cold to the touch? Etc. etc. THEN, why are you there? Start your story.

The chances are about 100% that you will end up NOT using that first paragraph anyway. But you get started.

Some "Easy Writing Tips" tell you to outline your whole book before you start. For me that's hogwash for fiction writers. Outlining a book is a tough procedure. Ask any college student. Plus, it takes all the spontaneity out of your project. Fiction is life. Life is unpredictable.

If you're recounting something that actually happened to you, you're going to probably tell your story in the first person, after all it's your story. In writing a book you may find it easier and more expressive to write as if you were a bystander, in the third person. In the first person you're limited to one person's viewpoint. In the third person, you have the advantage of viewing the happenings from any number of viewpoints. However, it's not terribly important at the beginning. As you continue your story, you will probably fall into one style or the other and then you can make changes retroactively.

Don't even think about it now, *just tell your story.*

OR
I'm speaking about my books at a book signing event and a person comes up to me and asks if he can speak to me personally for a few minutes about a writing problem he's having. A little later he tells me his problem. He has this great idea for a book but can't seem to get started. He has what I call, "first page-itis"

I ask him to "tell me about the story."

"It's about a guy that's accused of murdering his boss. He loses his job and has to prove his innocence."

"Okay. Now pretend YOU are the innocent employee and I'm your brother John. Tell me what's going on."

"John, I'm really scared. The police think I murdered my boss and I know damn well I didn't. But I think maybe I know who did. And, I don't know what to do."

"Okay, there's your first line. What you told me verbally. Just write it down as if it just came out of your character's mouth. Exactly as you would have talked to your brother. Now you're trapped. You have to explain the first sentence. You have to link it to the rest of the story. You're off and running."

Just write the damn thing, **just write the damn thing,** <u>just write the damn thing!</u>

It doesn't matter what you say, you'll probably change it later anyway. Start with something stupid, don't waste days or weeks searching for the perfect opening. Fiction isn't planned, it just happens, like life. What you wrote yesterday dictates what you will probably write today. The story writes itself. You create an impossible scenario for your hero today and spend the next 2 restless nights awake trying to figure a way out of the dilemma.

That's okay, maybe even necessary. The important thing is to open the flood gates. Don't worry about that wonderful first paragraph, it will come. Somebody said, "Fiction is just a bunch of lies." If necessary, start with an out and out lie.

A supposedly true story is that when GONE WITH THE WIND was first shown to anyone by Margaret Mitchell, it consisted of a box full of random notes. Let that be a lesson to all of us. She told a great story, someone else put it all together.

<u>MORAL:</u> *Chapterize* later, much later. Right now we're just talking, except its *IN PRINT!!* Maybe pretend you're writing a friendly letter to your best friend. Whatever it takes to get past that dreaded first page, then tell your story.

Now we've eliminated a big problem. You don't have to organize your story in chapters and create chapter headings. This will become even more valuable later on when you make inevitable changes in the text and foul up all the chapter numbers anyway.

A NOTE ABOUT NON-FICTION

This is where having done a book proposal – which essentially is a detailed outline of the book – really helps with non-fiction. Of course, until you finalize the text for publication, you can always move things around. This is something you will often find yourself doing when writing non-fiction unless you're following some chronology. Having a proposal with all the separate parts already laid out allows for an easy shuffling of those parts.

JUST WRITE THE DAMN THING !!

If Necessary, <u>STEP 4</u>

How to Block Writer's Block

***ACCORDING TO WEBSTER*: Writer's block** is a "condition, primarily associated with writing, in which an author loses the ability to produce new work."

A common cause of writer's block is a simple temporary loss of critical memory at a critical time. You can't remember an idea or a name or the name of a certain town or perhaps an important item. You bog down. You spend precious time agonizing over just the right idea or word. You lose your train of thought. Time goes by. You're stuck. What to do?

Answer? Ignore the problem. Simply and completely put it out of your mind. How? 5 red XXXXX's!

Hit your space bar a half dozen times then type in 5 red XXXXX's and plow ahead with your writing. You know that the missing name, place, idea or whatever will come to you eventually. When it does, go to FIND. Enter the 5 red XXXXX's. Go to site, erase the XXXXX's. Fill in the blank. Voila!

Usually I find the missing word or idea pops in a short time and I simply go back and fix it.

KEEP IT SIMPLE AND KEEP IT GOING!

<u>A NOTE ABOUT NON-FICTION</u>

Writer's block is certainly an issue when writing non-fiction as much as with fiction, but it's important to figure out what the block relates to.

For example, it could be simply that the chapter/section you're working on is missing information you can't pull from your brain, can't find in your notes, or still need to research. As Richard mentions above, put in a place holder and come back to that chapter or section later – work on a different, easier, part of the book.

Or it could be that you're too tired or too distracted to write at that moment. In that case, even if you're following a rigid schedule to write, put the book aside and get refreshed. Do something to alleviate the tiredness or low energy (you know, like get some sleep!). Do something fun, something that would bring you laughter, joy, energy. Meditate or get some exercise or physical activity. Then come back to the writing.

You'll find that rather than fighting the block in the moment, putting aside the writing will push away the writer's block. It may change your writing schedule (if you have one at all), but in the short and long run, the book (and you) will be better for it.

SECTION TWO:

EDITING

So finally, you have a book. It's not ready for publication or printing. You're not sure you want anyone to see it. What do you do?

First, if you have any money at all to invest in your book, before putting it on Amazon put it into proof-reading.

Nothing puts a reviewer off more than grammartical and smelling error after error. AND, it's very true that proof reading your own masterpiece is diffigult, diffigult, diffigult. (See?)

BUT, if you simply cannot afford the cost for proof-reading, what can you do? **Do it yourself!**

SELF EDITING OR PROOFING METHODS

It's commonly accepted wisdom that an author cannot proof-read or edit his own book. It's humanly impossible, they say. **BUT**, if you cannot afford or simply don't want to pay someone else to proof-read you novel, there are at least 3 ways I've found where you **CAN** proof read your own work. And **YOU** can do it. They're effective, cheap and easy. As follows:

FIRST: Buy a new or used copy of Patricia T. O'Conner's *Woe Is I*. That will humorously answer all your questions about commas, apostrophes, quotation marks etc. Simple, direct and cheap. Probably available at any used book store, or on Amazon. Or buy a new or used copy of *Eats, Shoots & Leaves* by Lynne Truss. Same as above.

SECOND:-The following takes time but it works. The reason you have trouble proof-reading your own book is that you read right over the errors. The reason you read right over them is that you see the whole sentence or paragraph.

SOLUTION? On your computer, blow up the page so large only a few words or sentences can be seen at a time. You can then review almost word by word, or sentence or sentence. Keep your copy of *Woe Is I* beside you. You can spot mistakes and you don't get caught up in your book. Example: You have a quotation within a quotation, how do you treat it? The answer's in *Woe is I*. It takes time, but it does work for me, AND it's free.

THIRD: Print your book on fast-print. Find or make a piece of cardboard 8 ½" X 4". Starting on page 1 lay the piece of cardboard over the page, covering everything up to the top line. Gradually slide the piece of cardboard down the page, exposing one sentence, and ONLY one sentence, at a time. You're artificially tricking your mind to not get wrapped up in the story. You will spot most errors. Having read *Woe Is I* and having it next to you, you'll recognize and fix most errors. Time consuming and somewhat laborious, but it works, it's free and it's effective.

OR
FOURTH: Read your book <u>out-loud</u> to someone. Most of your errors will be apparent as you read. Disadvantage? You may not recognize your own errors. Or use Natural Reader or other similar free software or apps, which are text to speech/voice programs for your computer.

OR
FIFTH: This is a neat idea, only available to self-publishers who use Print on Demand. When it looks pretty good to you, have a few books printed on POD. I like Amazon's <u>CreateSpace</u> (*www.createspace.com*). You can do it with or without a cover as a proof book. AND, you can make changes in subsequent printings for free. Cost to you? About $3.00-5.00 to buy a copy of your book, depending on the its size. Give those copies to your severest critics for errors, omissions and corrections. At this point, you could send copies to professional reviewers as advance copies, something mainstream publishers often do. It's the just of the cost of printing those books and shipping (and with CreateSpace, you can have each copy sent directly, which saves on postage). An extra expense but worth it.

When you've made all the suggested changes, you'll have a pretty well "proof-read" book.

What I did was to enter into a contract with CreateSpace at that stage and had 5 books printed, errors and all, in order to make it easy for others to read it and correct it for future printings. Also I wanted to see what it looked like in print. I wanted to get reaction from friends. Then I made the corrections, had 5 more printed and did it again. It was the 3rd edition that won prizes.

Several things you can try. You can read it out-loud to yourself or friends and see if it hangs together. A ream or two of paper is a cheap cost for a review. You can run off several copies and ask friends to read them and comment. Compare it to your running log. Move your paragraphs around. Improve on weak writing sections. Ask for help.

See if you can find a retired English teacher/professor and talk him/her into proof-reading your book for free. I found a wonderfully qualified lady that does mine, just for the enjoyment of being the first to see my work. In fact, there are a lot of people who love to be "first." It's just a matter of making sure they are qualified to do a good job!

Are there obvious gaps or errors? Encourage honest and brutal commentary. Even better would be two or more proofreaders.

Punctuation errors are insidious. Even the best miss some. One friend of mine is dyslectic and jokes that he could be the perfect proof-reader, as he almost has to read word by word. Maybe? You want the book to be a good one. If your reader is able and willing to comment on the editorial content also, so much the better. At one point a reviewer said "He never saw a comma he wasn't in love with."

If you do it yourself you need to research, research, and research. It takes time. It took me two years and I still find errors in the book that won prizes.

A PROFESSIONAL EDITOR IS ALWAYS BEST, but could cost you $$. Take a look at Kboards Editor List (see resources). Check out E-bay, Craigslist and Goodreads for freelance editor ads. Take a look aty the classifieds in *Writers' Digest Magazine* and on their website. Ask to see samples of their works. Some of them are as good as any and are nearby so you can interact personally with them. Challenge them to do an outstanding job and advance their credentials.

In any event, be sure to have at least one other person read the book, if only to be sure it flows well, the characters are interesting, and the story makes sense.

A NOTE ABOUT NON-FICTION

The above advice about editing applies to non-fiction as well. However, be sure to find someone who is interested (and perhaps even a little knowledgeable) in your subject area as your content editor.

SECTION 3

PUBLISHING

On to the finish line or,

THANK GOD FOR CREATESPACE.

WHAT ABOUT THE COVER?
WHAT ABOUT FORMATTING?
HOW MUCH DOES IT COST TO HAVE A BOOK PRINTED?

CHAPTERIZING
Now, finally, the time has come to start defining and labeling your chapters. You've made all the necessary changes in the text and you can make decisions about cliff-hanging chapter divisions. Don't worry about how short or long the chapters are as long as you try to keep the breaks logical and absolutely suspenseful. Once more, don't agonize over them.

COVERS
There are a number of stock pictures available on the computer. Some are free, such as what you can find on Shutterstock.com (Go to the site, type in subject and there you are). You can download a picture and use it for your cover.
CreateSpace now has a free cover creator, with its own templates, clip art, and stock photo. You can even upload your own photos into the cover creator.

COST:
Except for extras like professional cover design, editing and formatting, the initial cost of printing a book by CreateSpace, is only what you pay for books you personally buy. They make money on sales of your book but will charge you for extras if you choose to use their services. My first book sells at $12.49 and I can buy them for myself at $4.83 from CreateSpace. That cost is based on the size of the book. Mine now had 106,000 words. (328 pages)

FORMATTING:

CreateSpace will lead you thru the process. They will give you a template and loads of directions plus a consultant on phone or e-mail and guaranteed 24 hour response. Definitely do-able if you're patient. Once you decide to use CreateSpace, you'll get an ID #, and be able to set up a call with them for help 24/7. Their "Help" area has both frequently asked questions and a way to get either an email response or have one of their reps call you within a few minutes.

DON'T BE AFRAID TO CONTACT CREATESPACE AT ANY TIME!!!! Wow!!

OR

Go to Craig's List or do a search in Google and look for people who do book formatting. They're there and they're local. Check their credentials and bargain. But...

With the CreateSpace format templates, the actual formatting is pretty easy if you have minor skills with Word, especially when working with CreateSpace's customer help.

PRINTING:

There are places in China and India (China seems to be a little cheaper than India) that will do a good job of printing your prepared book for less than $3.00 per book, much less if you order a lot. I believe that many of the giant publishers have their books printed in China or India. PROBLEM: You have to buy books in volume. Usually a minimum of 1,000. Some sources will do as few as 500. MANY such companies are easily researched by going to *ALIBABA.COM*. They are easy to work with and respond quickly with quotes and service. Many to choose from.

U.S. and Canadian companies also will publish either in volume, small press runs, or P.O.D. (P.O.D. stands for Print on Demand.) Many companies offer this choice. If you order one book, they print one book and are able to deliver the book in overnight shipping. It's more expensive and less profitable per book, but relieves you of the responsibility of having a garage full of unsold books.

AN ADDITIONAL BIG ADVANTAGE! You can make changes in your book as you discover mistakes etc. for free. The very next book printed will be mistake free. (At least of the ones you just corrected)

HOWEVER, at the risk of sounding like a shill for CreateSpace, I still think they are the best, easiest to work with and most effective of all publishing companies.

PUBLISHING:

BE CAREFUL!!

If you Google "Book Publishers," besides mainstream publishers (ones that would be listed in _Writer's Market_ or on the **_www.WritersMarket.com_** website), there are dozens and dozens of book packagers and internet-based publishers out there. Most of them are not worth a tinker's damn. Many of them are outright crooks.

They will lure you with "mail or email your book, if we find it acceptable, we will mail you a contract." Guess what, they're all acceptable. A few years ago a group of authors cobbled together a horrible novel on purpose to test one of these companies. It was accepted. Next step, mail money.

Legitimate publishers say NEVER, NEVER pay $$$ up front to a publisher (a printer is different). They should pay you. If you're intrigued you can check out this site, _www.writerbeware.com,_ or email them at for a direct and specific answer. They list dangerous and dishonest publishers and are being sued for being so direct and honest. Another source is Predators & Editors (_http://pred-ed.com_). It lists many editors and agents and highlights the bad ones.

My personal recommendation, which you've seen before, is CreateSpace (_www.createspace.com_), a division of Amazon.com. They're dependable, reasonable, experienced and honest. ALSO, they're reachable by phone, day or night. Remarkable!! I am very happy with the quality of their finished product, my books. Check them out on-line. Don't be afraid to call them at the phone number on their site. Ask questions. Have them explain their services. You'll be pleasantly surprised at how simple the process is.

You follow their step by step process. You start a title, add in the ISBN number (see below), choose a trim (book) size and paper. You upload the file, and set up the cover (either your own or through their Cover Creator).You submit the interior and cover files. They make sure there are no formatting problems and tell you that an electronic proof is ready (or that there are problems you may or may not need to fix). You review the proof on CreateSpace online, or download it (and you can print it if you need to). You approve it or fix the errors and re-upload (and wait for new approval).

Once you approve the proof, it's ready to go.

You price the book.

You choose where it's going to be distributed on Amazon.com (US & Canada only? Europe? India? Everywhere?) Through other online booksellers (at a lower royalty of course)?

Launch it! It will be up on Amazon.com in a very few short days (or sooner).

You can decide at that point (or later) to send the book over to Kindle Direct and have it published as a Kindle ebook.

Simple!

Note: You can always order a few copies of the book before making it "live" on Amazon.com. These copies can be given to folks who might proof-read for you, or to advance reviewers, or just to your friends. Get feedback from them, challenge them to find errors, then fix the errors, redo the file and proof, approve it and let it go "live"!

ISBN:
You should get an ISBN number. BOWKER is the official source of ISBN numbers. The ISBN number is the number seen on the cover of every book you buy. It allows the book to be tracked and found. You can identify a book with separate ISBN numbers for your e-book and for your bound book.

Your publisher, (CreateSpace, for example) can get both for you. HOWEVER, there are limitations on its usage if you use CreateSpace. If you ever need another publisher for any reason, you will have to get another ISBN.

Use BOWKER. (U.S. ISBN Agency) If you are the *only* author and copyright owner and if the book is completely new, use FORM – TX. The BOWKER ISBN can be used by any publisher.

NOTE. If you intend to publish only thru Amazon and CreateSpace, you save money.

Bowker: $125.00

CreateSpace, $0.00 (Zero)

BIG CAVEAT. If you want to ever have your books in bookstores you may want to investigate INGRAM/SPARK publishers. Just about every bookstore in the US buys their books from them, not Amazon. Amazon has a new program to get their books into limited stores.

LCCN:
Your publisher is the only organization that can acquire a LCCN for you, and they will do it for you automatically. LCCN? LIBRARY OF CONGRESS CONTROL NUMBER. It's a reference to the catalog number. I don't bother with it.

COPYRIGHT:
You may want to get an official U.S. copyright for your book through the U.S. Copyright Office. Forms and information available online. Just go to *www.copyright.gov* and follow simple instructions. You'll save money filing it online ($35) vs. the cost of using paper forms, $85.00. If you need help you can contact them directly.

However, as soon as you print the book or get it out as an e-book, you do have copyright protection from a legal standpoint. US Copyright protection does make it easier to address issues of plagiarism.

E-BOOKS:

Nowadays, you must publish your book as an e-book as well as in print. But there are many formats, and you need to decide which one or ones. If you use Amazon/CreateSpace as your only e-book printer, you will be only on Kindle. How many suppliers are there? Answer: I-Pad, Amazon, Barnes & Noble (Nook), Smashwords, Baker & Taylor, Reader, Kobo, Book Pie, Copia, and GB are some. Why not get on all of them?

BOOK BABY (www.bookbaby.com) can do that for you. Depending on whether you want to give them a little split of the royalties, you can get basic services for free up to $99. Cheap! They have a number of services available, and a blog with excellent information and advice that goes well beyond what Book Baby provides. My preference for cost containment, Kindle and Nook only. VERY little cost (actually, pretty much zero cost up front).

A LITTLE BIT ON MARKETING YOUR BOOK

The next section, by Loyd Auerbach, is really going to provide a great foundation for marketing yourself and your book. But here's a little bit I've learned...

REVIEWS:

Reviews are a necessity in order to market your books these days. Often the marketing sites on the Web won't accept a book unless it has at least a 4 star average review on Amazon. Right or wrong, people buy based on numbers of reviews and star average. Whoever reviews your book should make sure they are on every site your readers might go to. That should include Amazon, Goodreads etc.

GOODREADS.COM:

A great site. Join it. Primarily designed for book buyers but a great place for authors too. Discussion groups, advertising opportunities, source for help for authors, but use it correctly. Read books and report on them. Get active in groups –make your presence known.

GOODREADS GIVEAWAYS:

Give away finished galleys or pre-release copies to book reviewers OR to a group from your e-mail list that have agreed to be test readers. They should be representative of a cross section and willing to make honest comments as well as reviews. Ask them for reviews, comments and improvements.

PAID FOR REVIEWS:

Many look down their noses at paid for reviews. However many reviews are paid for one way or another. If the book reviewed is provided by the author, that's pay. Where the line should be drawn is if the reviewer promises a 4 or 5 star review in return for pay. There are a number of legitimate sources offering honest reviews online. You are free to post their review wherever you wish.

Almost all require payment; many do *not* guarantee results except that you may have the right to stop the distribution of a negative review. Many will only review if the book is made available at your expense. You can get somewhat questionable but inexpensive reviews from *Fiverr.com*.

You might send your book to one or more *PROFESSIONAL REVIEWERS*. You can find lots of them online. Pick one with a good reputation and that fits your budget. This may cost you a few dollars, but it can be valuable. You will get an honest and tough review. They will not pull their shots. Very, very few authors get a really good review. They will probably disappoint your expectations. It doesn't matter. You can profit from their criticism. Usually, they'll let you correct things that generated their criticisms and re-submit your corrected book for a 2nd and hopefully happier review. Usually for free.

Best result for you? You will own the review outright. You can quote from it and attribute the quote to the Professional Reviewer. Your quote can be any part of the review you wish. Choose only the best part!! You can quote from or use in entirety on Facebook etc.

SUMMARY

Every word in my booklet is true, though sometimes website information needs to be updated. Every bit of advice I've given, I've used successfully. I challenge you to use my plan, my ideas, if you're serious about becoming an author. Writing a book is not a mysterious project. It's simply, writing a book. There should be no mystery to it. Most of the problems prospective authors fear disappear in the face of common sense. That's all I did, apply common sense to the problem. Could I find a way to overcome the fear of beginning? Could I find a way to be my own editor? Could I find a way for me to be my own proof-reader? Could I be my own publisher? I decided I could and therefore I did.

Sometimes, ignorance is bliss. If you were not aware of all those typographical and English language rules, you could just sit down and write your novel. You wouldn't be stymied. I'm trying to contribute to your ignorance and therefore help you to be successful.

So there you have it. Seems too simple, doesn't it. How come others don't use these ideas? Maybe they do.

All I know is that they worked for me when I needed them, and I never saw them in print before. I did talk to one aspiring author that told me her college literary professor had told her to just wade into her novel and not worry about punctuation etc. There is nothing new in the world.

You <u>CAN</u> write that novel. Decide you can and do it. Keep it simple and write it. You <u>CANNOT</u> make a mistake. It's <u>YOUR</u> book. <u>YOU</u> make all the final decisions. I'd wish you the best of luck, but luck has nothing to do with it. It's just common sense and perseverance. The sooner you start, the more you write, the easier it gets.

The only hard cost for publishing a book this way is really the cost of the copies you order, unless you do US Copyright, which right now, filing electronically and with a single author, is $35.00.

I welcome any comments or questions you may have. My website and blog site is *POOR RICHARD PUBLISHERS BLOG* (*http://www.rlwren.com/*)

My e-mail is **r.wren@sbcglobal.net**

REMEMBER YOUR NEW MOTTO:

JUST WRITE THE DAMN THING !!

A SOUP-CON OF STUFF

(A miscellaneous mélange of worthwhile suggestions)

1) All fiction should reflect LIFE. Human's experience accidents, disease, adversities, death, failure, success, ups and downs, wars, etc. etc., in varying degrees. So should your characters. Let bad and unexpected things happen.

2) Flaw your characters. Nobody's perfect and we're all different. How is your character different? A limp, a stutter, a mental quirk, an unusual history. Something to make him memorable.

3) Make your character suffer. Make him overcome adversity. The more he or she suffers, the more your reader will his enjoy his victories. Building up his problems make the solution more exciting. Makes your book a page turner.

4) Use what I call "discovery writing." (not a phrase I coined) In your mind you have a sympathetic lead character. You put him into a dangerous situation. You have no idea how he overcomes it. You imagine yourself in that position with your characters abilities. How to get out?? You need to DISCOVER a solution. In other words, where you left your character yesterday forces you to discover what he does today. JUST LIKE LIFE, yesterday predicts today. Yesterday's page predicts today's page.

5) Use alliteration, metaphors, synonyms, etc., to taunt, titillate, treat, tease, target and torment your reader. Use The Synonym Finder and Roget.

6) Set your story in a location you're extremely familiar with. Use your unique knowledge of the area to your advantage. Describe places intimately.

7) Leave something to your reader's imagination. Not every detail is necessary. It's not a text, it's an imaginary story. Trust your readers.

8) The computer age adage: "Butt in chair, hands on keyboard."

JUST WRITE THE DAMN THING !!

RESOURCES

Alibaba book printing:
http://www.alibaba.com/showroom/overseas-book-printing.html

Avoid Scams (P & E article) **http://critters.org/c/pubtips.ht?t1**

Book Publisher List: (P & E list) **http://pred-ed.com/peba.ht**

Book Review Source:
http://authorsreading.com/book_review.php

Bowker ISBN & Barcode: **http://www.isbn-us.com/**
        Phone #: 1(800) 662-0701 (x250)

CreateSpace: **https://www.createspace.com/**
        Member phone #: 1 (866) 356-3154
CreateSpace Cover creator:
https://www.createspace.com/Tools/CoverCreator.jsp

Eats, Shoots & Leaves: **http://www.amazon.com/Eats-Shoots-Leaves-Tolerance-Punctuation/dp/1592402038**

Free Grammarly digital Proof Book:
http://www.grammarly.com
        (Make own PDF copy for proofing)

Free ISBN (Create Space):
https://www.createspace.com/Products/Book/ISBNs.jsp

Goodreads: **https://www.goodreads.com/**

Ingram/Spark: **https://www.ingramspark.com/**

Kboards: **http://www.kboards.com/yp/**
Natural Reader: **Free text to voice.**
http://www.naturalreaders.com/

Nook. (Barnes & Noble) https://www.nookpress.com/

Phrase frequency finder:
http://www.writewords.org.uk/phrase_count.asp

Poor Richard Publishers: http://www.rlwren.com/

Preditors & Editors: http://pred-ed.com/

Richard L. Wren (author): http://www.rlwren.com/

Richard L. Wren (blog): http://www.rlwren.com/category/blog/

Shutterstock: http://www.shutterstock.com/photos

Types of editing defined:
http://www.selfpublishingadvice.org/editing-definitions/

U.S.Copyright Office: http://copyright.gov/forms/formtx.pdf
        Form TX. Phone # 1 (877) 476 0778
        Office Staff Member Phone # (202) 707-3000

"Woe Is I." http://www.amazon.com/Woe-Grammarphobes-Better-English-Edition/dp/157322331X

Word frequency finder:
http://www.writewords.org.uk/word_count.asp

Wrensense: http://www.rlwren.com/category/blog/

Wrensense U Tube: http://YouTube.com/richardlwren

Writer Beware: http://accrispin.blogspot.com/

PART TWO:

PROMOTION!

By

Loyd Auerbach, MS

SECTION 4

BOOK AND AUTHOR PROMOTION

Loyd Auerbach, M.S.

One of the attractive things about traditional publishers is that they may put some resources to promoting their authors and the books they publish. But this is an unrealistic expectation on the part of most authors.

I say "may put some resources" because unless the publisher sees a real sales potential for the book, there's little likelihood they will spend any money or even time to promote the book and author. As most books fall into this (not likely to be a bestseller) category, authors should not expect anything more than a reactive PR/marketing effort. In other words, while the publicity department/rep might send out copies of the book to reviewers, TV and radio interviewers, or reporters and well-known bloggers, this will usually be because of a request from the media outlet rather than because they are being proactive.

Consequently, it's been important for all but a small percentage of authors to expect to carry out their own promotion and publicity efforts, whether they do them for themselves (which cuts into your time and energy) or hire a publicist (which of course, cuts into your money). This is especially true of self-published authors, and authors with very small publishing houses.

Additionally, to even sell a book to many publishers, one needs to already have an author platform established. This means you have a media presence (radio, TV, magazine/newspaper – print or online – interviews, interviews by bloggers) and have demonstrated social media skills and preferably a good following on Facebook and Twitter especially. In other words, you have to have *presence* in the world.

The former presents a greater challenge for fiction writers than for nonfiction authors who might be experts in a field they are also writing about. The exception is people who are experts or celebrities or known for something they've done (that got them media attention) who are adding fiction to their repertoire of things they do.

Former (or current) law enforcement who write mysteries, psychics and mediums who write anything from mystery to science fiction to general fiction to paranormal romance, scientists who play out theoretical speculation from their own fields, artists who write stories around being an artist, and so on. They have the hook, in that their fiction is based on stuff they have practiced, worked at, know or are involved in.

In other words, fiction writers who bring real-life experience into their novels have a selling point beyond how wonderful their stories and characters and messages are.

As for something they've done in their lives, Richard Wren is a great example.

In his 80s, he decided to do something new: write a novel! In other words, he reinvented himself from a retiree to an author. Doing this in what so many would consider "late" in life – and especially now that he's published three novels with a fourth on the way – is a great hook (attention grabber).

Sometimes to journey to becoming an author can be the grabber that secures one's platform, as can writing about that journey in social media (a good blog, which can eventually even be turned into another book).

As for non-fiction writers, the subject itself can be the hook, especially if combined with expertise in that subject.

UTILIZING THE MEDIA FOR SELF PROMOTION
An Introduction

LOYD AUERBACH, M.S.

What do you mean by Media?

In this section of the book, I'll mainly be dealing with traditional Media (TV, radio, print newspapers, print magazines) and their internet-based offshoots/current formats (web-based video "shows," internet radio, podcasts, blogs, online newspapers and online magazines).

However, **Social Media** is especially important to both published (especially self-published) authors and wanna-be authors. Consequently, you'll find some basic commentary on using several social media services to both create your platform (your visibility) and to promote yourself and your projects.

Why do we need the Media?

The Media, whether traditional or online, and Social Media are undoubtedly the greatest influence on the consciousness of the individual, with perhaps the exception of our parents as we're growing up, and this has been the case for traditional Media for decades. The Media and the Internet/Web suffuses our environment, giving credibility and credence to all, whether such is intended or not. The Internet/Web can bring credibility or tear that credibility down.

Experts in any and all fields that deal with the general public need the Media as a venue for discussing issues in their fields. More than that, if the expert has a particular point of view to present -- or "sell" as some might say -- the Media becomes a vehicle for such presentation.

In addition, if that particular point of view is represented by products, whether articles, books, ebooks, audio, video, games, inventions, services or other money-generating items, the Media is an essential part of the sales effort.

Objectivity is difficult if not impossible to obtain in media reporting, since complete neutrality and total detachment from our emotional and mental biases is simply not human, and it seems that personal and corporate/network bias has become the norm. Reporting the news or absorbing the news is simply a subjective process that, consciously or unconsciously, affects our perceptions and judgments of the world around us.

All too often people have difficulty in feeling they are represented fairly and objectively. Instead, they may feel that the Media seems to be negatively reinforcing certain downsides of their professions or areas of expertise. Or, worse, the Media doesn't represent them at all.

This need not be, if one takes an active role with the Media in understanding just what it is that they want in a story and in working with them to achieve their ends without sacrificing one's own. Reporters and commentators need interesting stories -- that will catch people's eyes, ears and interests -- and need to present the stories in a fashion that will engage the reader, watcher or listener all the while bringing the Media source its business goals, sales and ratings.

In understanding the various Media, keep in mind that they, like you, are in *business.* They're not in it strictly as a public service – though with the advent of podcasting and webcasting video, there is an enormous (and growing) number of outlets that are not business ventures. The mainstream Media have sales to achieve, circulations and ratings to grow. Unfortunately, too many people forget this side of the Media and see only the end result of stories and interviews and not any part of the process behind why the story may have gotten screwed up (from the participant's point of view).

The Media can be a great help to the savvy author and speaker. By understanding three things, you can in a sense manipulate the Media rather than be manipulated by it. Those three things are:

1) Understanding the various Media and its methods, goals, the people involved, the audience being targeted, and the format of the final "package"

2) Understanding yourself and your subject or business or selling points (your "hook") so as to know how to package yourself as an "expert" or "spokesperson" or "personality"

3) Understanding how the Media has presented your subject or business or similar books/writing before

4) Understanding how you can present your message through the Media, based on the above, in a way that will capture the interest of the audience without sounding like a TV commercial (or one of the walking dead).

Why does the Media need people like you?

The various Media are always looking for interesting people who can provide them with new information and topics or new angles on old information and topics. They want people who know what they're talking about, yet at the same time, they often look for people who don't sound like a politician or fast-talking public relations person. They don't necessarily want the over-informed yet glib spokesperson, they want interesting people who can speak for themselves and talk *about* their subject or their field of endeavor or their company, rather than talking *for* it.

Who is an "expert" or qualified guest or interviewee? You are, provided you know what you're talking about, you're honest in your responses, you can be yourself when you speak, and you don't take yourself too seriously. If you have a good story to tell from your life, you are presenting yourself as an expert on YOU.

You can be trained, or in fact can train yourself, to be that "expert" and feel comfortable in interview situations. Having a professional publicist or P.R. representative is great, and often necessary. However, these are not necessarily the only people who should be in the spotlight or who you need to get you the spotlight, though they can make things much simpler and hassle-free. You may be just the sort of interesting individual who can impress the public with knowledge and sincerity, and who may be just that much more believable because you are *NOT* a P.R. person.

"Talent," therefore, can be those people like you who know their topics, who can speak in public without freezing up, and who come across as sincere, interesting people in their own right. Also, they are people who can remember that they are in Media-related situations to provide and interesting story or interview, not only to run an ad for something. They may not even be doing an interview to talk about their products/books/etc. or themselves (directly). But, their products/books/etc. or services or credentials are generally mentioned and such publicity for the products/books/services/etc. becomes a by-product of any successful Media encounter.

What is your Message?

Before you seek out the Media, you should have an idea of what you need -- and want -- to get across to the public. Pick one, two or three main points that you can expand on, and put them down on paper in a brief, succinct fashion. Lengthy answers to questions often lose their impact, and TV and Radio interviewers (and most podcast hosts) prefer your answers to be in succinct "sound bites." Your points can be interrelated or not. They should be points that don't give away everything, but are complete. They should lead to more questions.

Why lead to more questions?

If your aim is to get more Time or Space in the Media's outlets, you need to make them want to talk with you. Handing them an interesting, yet complete, story (everything you know and can say about it) is fine if you want to do their work for them for free.

However, it's better to give them something they can use as a base point, a place to start with their own questions, since they are hopefully anticipating the kinds of questions their audience might ask. You want to give them enough to tantalize, yet not enough to fulfill.

You also want to try to anticipate other angles, other paths for follow-up of the story or idea, so that a month -- or a year -- down the road they might find they can come back to you for an update, for a new and interesting way to look at your topic, or for your commentary on a related issue or incident.

This is not to say that you can't present them with a particular incident, anecdote, or application within your area of expertise. For example, you can tell the entire story of one of your clients, co-workers, friends or relatives, or one situation you've been in personally.

Your short points can be made in the form of an announcement, a press release, or can be made in a short biographical sketch of you, the "expert," who is sending the bio out to the Media to announce your availability for interview or consultation on certain topics or issues.

One way to make yourself "available" is to know others in your area of expertise or related areas. You can make yourself quite useful to the Media if you can suggest others to interview, even those with opposing viewpoints (provided such opposition is respected by you and is fair in his/her treatment of the issue as well).

If you are knowledgeable in a subject that has broader implications for the public than just what you do or say or write about, stick as much as you can with that topic in your contacts with the Media. This makes you more of an "expert." It makes you more likely to be called on commentary on the issue/topic and related issues/topics, and the mere fact that your name and your writing or other product is mentioned gives the appropriate kind of promotional press, and often better promotion because you're not perceived as "advertising."

PRESS KIT: Consider making these pieces downloadable on your website.

The basic pieces you might send out/have available are as follows. You should learn as much as you can about how to write these.

1. The Press Release -- when something is happening, whether the release of a new book or product, the announcement of a meeting, the announcement of some conclusion reached, etc. It also makes for good fodder for Social Media postings (Facebook, Twitter, Google+, LinkedIn, etc.).

2. The Paid Wire Story/Release -- you can pay to have a story or press release sent across various wire services. There are many ways to get press releases out there, thanks to the internet. A couple of major promotional services are Business Wire and PRNewswire, and you can find individuals who help with distribution on those and other wire services by searching services like www.fiverr.com.

3. The Short Bio(graphical Sketch) -- learn to write several versions of a short biographical sketch: one complete (that may be as long as two pages), one that might fit on a book cover (in a paragraph or two) and one that works as an introduction of you when you're speaking or being interviewed. You'll need this for your website anyway (it's the "About" page on your site).

4. The List of Topics of Expertise or Referral -- make a list of all the topics and subtopics you can speak to.

5. The Lecture Brochure or One-Sheet for those who do public speaking

6. Frequently Asked Questions piece (FAQ)

7. A list of questions for interviewers to ask, about both your topic(s) and you.

8. One-sheet(s) on your main topic(s)

9. The Website url and Social Media page urls

Who and What is the Media?

Before doing anything else, it is important to understand who you are approaching (or who is approaching you), what their position with the particular Media means in the context of what they might want from you, and how you and your subject has been (in the past) and might be (in the present and future) presented through them to the public.

If you are a writer, you may already understand the functions of folks in the print Media, but it doesn't hurt to refresh that knowledge. You may have written for television or radio or film, or at least watched and listened to quite a bit, but do you understand the function of, say, a producer for a film vs. a TV producer vs. a radio talk show producer?

As this piece I have written is an introduction and somewhat of a guideline, I won't be explaining all these positions to you here. It's up to you to do the background research on these positions especially for the specific media source. A simple Google search will give you the basics before even exploring the publication, show, network, website, etc.

Do a little background research on:

A. Newspapers -- various types: local, metropolitan area, college, national papers, tabloids, dailies and weeklies; free newspapers. Be sure to look at their online versions (since more is often published online than in print), and look for online-only newspapers/news sites as well.

B. Magazines: print-only, print/online, and online-only

C. Wire Services (AP, Reuters, Gannett Wire Service, PRNewswire, BusinessWire, etc.)

D. Newsletters -- from those published by organizations and associations to industries to corporations. Start online, but be sure to check websites for mentions of their print publications.

E. Radio (and the types of shows you find, similar to television). Note that there are plenty of stations/shows that simulcast on the web, as well as internet-only radio "stations."

F. Television
1. "Free" broadcast TV (general broadcast; the major networks and local stations)
2. Cable/Satellite TV: Networks that aren't broadcast other than via cable/satellite systems – in other words, almost all of them
3. NEWS programs (and the difference between "hard" and "soft" news)
4. TV MAGAZINE shows, which offer many segments about different topics in the same show
5. EDUCATIONAL TV and Video (including Public Broadcasting)
6. TALK shows
7. ENTERTAINMENT shows
8. PUBLIC AFFAIRS programming
9. Web-based TV and Video shows, "stations," and even "networks"

G. THE INTERNET / WORLD WIDE WEB as Media Provider
1. NEWS sites
2. TOPICAL sites -- organizations, newsletters, online magazines, newspapers, and newsletters
3. WEBCASTING sites: radio over the Internet
4. PODCASTING sites: everybody has them, it seems, and more and more people are getting them. There are a number of podcast "networks" (like BlogTalkRadio and Libsyn)
5. BLOGS
6. SOCIAL NETWORKING sites like Facebook and Twitter (more in a bit)

To further work through who to contact, break down the people and their positions for your sources. This is mainly for example purposes, and is hardly complete. Not all positions relate to all Media or publications, and many titles/positions have been added to online media:
A. Print Media
1. Editors

        a. Executive Editor
        b. Managing Editor
        c. City Editor
        d. Sunday/Weekend Editor(s)
        e. Features Editor
        f. Section Editors
        g. Photo Editor
        h. Fiction Editor
        i. Special Assignments Editor

2. Writers
        a. Reporters
        b. Staff Writers
        c. Free-Lancers
        d. Editorial Writers
        e. Beat Writers/Reporters
        f. Bureaus
            i. Bureau Chief
            ii. Correspondents
            iii. Stringers
        g. Columnists
        h. Copy Writers
        i. Bloggers

B. Electronic/Broadcast Media (may be very different for Radio and TV and vastly different for internet media providers)

    1. Directors
    2. Assignment Editors
    3. Producers
        a. News
        b. Special Features/Documentary
        c. Talk Show
        d. Independent Producers
    4. Associate Producers
    5. Assistant Producers
    6. Production Assistant
    7. Researchers
    8. Public Affairs Directors
    9. Talent Coordinators

10. Hosts

Learn who these people are and what their relationships to their publications/shows/networks are.

C. The Internet/World Wide Web and Social Media: Compared to the long history of Broadcast Media and the even longer history of Print Media, online media outlets and Social Media services/sources represent a relatively new – and ever-changing – bunch of venues for experts. You should absolutely get your own website up and running, since that's one place you can put all your press materials. People and the Media will find you through your website, and you can refer them to your website to learn more about you and your subject.

The traditional positions of producers and editors may be supplanted by "webmasters" or others. However, most of the sites that effectively webcast interview shows do tend to have producers and hosts. Some hosts of internet-based radio and podcasting do their interviews by phone, while an increasing number are doing interviews via Skype and similar services (both voice-only and video/voice combinations).

[Note: Broadcast radio shows typically want to interview you on the ever-disappearing "land line."]

What do you do if the Media calls for an interview?

There are a few things to consider when contacted for interviews or comments, and a few ways to handle the initial contact. In the event of a request from the Media, consider the following:

1) What is the focus of the piece/show? What kind of questions will be asked?

2) Why is the piece/show topic being done now? What is the timing of it and how will it be tied into other stories? What are those other stories? If TV, how much airtime will be devoted to it? How much time will be spent taping? (this last is relates to getting some idea as to how much editing will be done)

3) Who else is to be interviewed for the piece/show?

4) Who is the interviewer? Does he or she have a particular interest in the topic?

5) Live or pre-recorded? (TV or Radio or Internet Webcast/Podcast) If pre-recorded, will it be broadcast without editing? Will it be available (and how long) for downloading?

6) Who is the audience? How much of an audience is there? (Especially important for podcasts).

The above questions will yield information that will give you a better feel for whether the piece is entirely appropriate for you and your schedule. Remember, however, that you can offer suggestions, that the focus of the piece is entirely subject to change, that questions can be altered, especially if your ideas are as interesting (or hopefully more-so) than what is told to you. Also keep in mind that you can suggest appropriate areas for exploration that are better suited to your own expertise, and that you can suggest others to be interviewed who might compliment your own viewpoints.

Also consider some logistical and other issues:

1) How much time is to be involved?

2) When and where will the interview take place?

3) Are you physically and mentally available for the time, place and duration of the interview?

Think how great it is to do interviews via phone or Skype! Then again, if you're on the West Coast and someone is wanting to interview you for a 7 AM Eastern time radio show or podcast, do you want to do the interview at 4 AM Pacific? And will you be awake enough for it?

4) Do you *want* to do it? If you get a hunch that the interview is not appropriate, it's often best to say "no," though with an explanation and even better, a referral to someone who might be more appropriate.

Turning down an interview is not the end of the world, but it's best to avoid the "no" answer unless absolutely necessary (for example, because of scheduling conflicts or simply because you are not the "right" person for the piece). If you know for a fact that the journalist is a complete bungler, that his/her publication/show is exploitive and unfair, or you know he/she is going to be personally critical or hostile due to personal opinions, you may need to turn the interview down (be diplomatic!). But be honest in your refusal, unless you get any inkling that doing so will cause more harm. You might say something like "I just don't feel my work would get fair treatment, based on other pieces you've done in relation to this subject."

Keep in mind that sometimes pieces portray a subject badly because either the journalist is misinformed or because the "expert" interviewed previously was uninformed, or not quite the expert the journalist thought. You may do a great service for yourself, your chosen field and subject, and everyone else involved in your field or industry, if you spend a bit of time educating the unknowing journalist. Enlighten the person and be patient in that process. It often pays to do this even if you are not going to do the piece, since the journalist may be more appreciative of you and your position, and will hopefully come back later with a more appropriate piece or interview (or will refer you to someone else more appropriate).

Keeping your thoughts together and how to face the Interview:
It's okay to be a bit nervous. This gets the adrenaline going. Performers often speak of being more worried when they're not nervous at all, since the nervousness keeps them on top of the situation, and the lack of it may mean they're not paying attention to what they're doing enough to perform well (or in an interesting manner). No nerves may lead to boredom -- if they're bored, so is the audience.

But don't focus on being nervous. That will only make you more nervous. Focus on your knowledge. Pay attention to the following when facing the Interview:

1) Prepare yourself. Plan out three or four points you need to get across (be succinct!) and maybe some sub-issues. Try to discuss them with the interviewer before getting underway. For a print interview, bring them up right away and say these points are appropriate.

2) Provide the interviewer about you and your points beforehand. A short biography helps them ask the right questions, as does a short list of questions (you've prepared) or a list of sub-topics and related topics you can address. Many interviewers will ask you in advance for these.

3) Know who the audience is. Plan your message and your language appropriately. Don't talk over the heads of the audience, but don't speak down to them either.

4) Anticipate the interviewer's questions from what you had discussed previously about the piece/interview, and from the line of questioning in the interview. Be ready for "surprise" questions and be ready to always stay calm.

5) Be aware that you may meet some skepticism or downright disbelief, no matter what your subject is. Be prepared in that you need to stay calm and not get sucked in to any emotional arguments (against or for your views). This is especially important if your "opponent" gets insulting.

Guests who keep their cool, even when under fire, can gain the sympathy of the audience – especially if the host (or other guest, if that's where the "attack" is coming from) starts losing his/her cool.

6) Don't assume the interviewer is the "enemy," even if there are a few tough questions. If you are too much on the defensive, it'll show, and you will make yourself a target -- or you'll make a few blunders without the interviewers help.

7) Be as candid as you can, open and honest and sincere. If you don't know the answer to a question, admit it -- don't bluff. You can say, however, something like "I don't know the answer now, but I can certainly try to find out for you."

If the information the interviewer is asking about is confidential, say so. Don't beat around the bush. They'll respect you for it.

Try to avoid the "no comment" approach.

Don't speculate unless you make it clear that this is what you're doing.

Offer your opinion as just that: An Opinion. If you need to, offer a disclaimer with reference to others in your field/company/business: "I'm not sure what others might say, but my opinion is..."

8) Be Yourself. Speak naturally and use the same colorful phrases you might use when speaking with friends. Embellish your speech, but don't make it too flowery (or crude). You do want to be quotable.

Relax, smile, sit comfortably in the chair (though try to lean forward just a touch -- makes it look like you're paying attention rather than falling asleep).

Don't use technical jargon, or, if you must, follow the word immediately with a very brief definition/explanation.

9) Be Enthusiastic, even a bit dramatic, about your topic. Emotion is contagious. So is boredom. Express the same enthusiasm that keeps you interested in your topic.

10) Be Natural. Move your hands if you feel like it, especially in trying to make specific points. Movement helps you look alive, less scared to be there. On the other hand, be conscious of repetitive movements or gestures.

11) Be Specific. Bring in people, places and things where you can.

12) Use Anecdotes, stories, and analogies. People react better when they have a vested interest in something, so try to draw a connection between your topic and the audience's experiences.

13) Be Current. Show that what you're talking about has a current and future affect, and is happening right now.

14) Use Humor but don't try to be funny! A humorous, light-hearted attitude wins over the audience.

     Don't tell jokes and don't even try to be a stand-up comic. Stay away from jokes and one-liners unless they are spontaneously generated by the situation (in which case you may be better off not avoiding them).

     Puns pop up often. Don't miss out. People may groan, but even that is a clear sign that they were paying attention (and groaners have a habit of repeating the puns to others).

     Do tell amusing (*relevant*) anecdotes.

     Being able to not take yourself, or your subject, too seriously is a good thing. Being able to laugh at yourself is a sign of maturity and really wins over an audience. If you make a funny faux pas, laugh with the audience (even if it's *at* you) -- at least smile and show you're not stopped or put off by it.

15) YOU can direct the interview. When you are not finished with a point, don't let the interviewer butt in (unless the show has to go to commercial, and then make sure you can finish the point when you're back on the air).

     However, always be aware of what you are saying and be *succinct and brief.* An interviewer may have to stop you from running off at the mouth (don't be long winded!)

16) You can choose not to answer all or part of a question. But rather than a flat refusal, try to use that question as a starting point for another point you'd like to make. Expand on something you've already said.

     Feel free to redirect the interview with a new topic or point (but be ready to provide a transitional statement so the audience won't feel a break in your logic).

17) Don't let an interviewer goad you into speaking more than you need to.

Some interviewers like to use *silence* as a way to get you to keep talking beyond when you are done with an answer or point. When you're done, stop.

It's the interviewer's job to keep the interview going in a lively fashion. If there's silence, it's HIS or HER job to break that silence first, especially on radio (that's called "dead air"). Don't let the silent trapper get you.

Of course, you could use the silence to launch into a new point or topic.

18) If events happen unexpectedly, or surprise guests show up, try not to be flustered. But you may let the audience know that it IS a surprise to you.

19) There are no such things as statements "off the record." While most reporters and interviewers will respect such comments and their restrictions, you can never really tell...

20) Try to avoid negative phrases or repeating the interviewer's questions or words when phrased in a negative way.

21) If the interviewer repeats back what you said, make sure the rephrasing is accurate. If not, say so and make a correction immediately.

22) Don't use all your material. Always leave them wanting a little more, by throwing out hints of other pertinent information you may have to provide at a later date. Give suggestions during the interview for related topics that would be of future interest. This gets you back for other interviews (if you did well the first time).

23) Be aware that (or when) you may be edited. Offer your help in checking accuracy of quotes or facts before the story goes to press, or before it is finished with final editing.

24) *KNOW WHAT YOU'RE TALKING ABOUT,* and be confident that you do!! It shows!

25) Keep on top of the Media's coverage of your topic – and how it's showing up on Social Media – as well as similar and related topics and other experts or commentators on your field, subject or topic. The more current you stay with the attitudes toward your subject matter, the better prepared you'll be. This will also suggest new angles you can cover -- by seeing what has already been done. The Media always likes to do *new* rather than rehash the old.

Use the Internet and other online services to keep on top of your subject. Remember to look carefully at the source of the information provided over the Net, since there's so much garbage out there (Remember to check facts, since people may post false or misleading information on purpose or innocently pass it on from other sources, and then there are those who simply post from ignorance of a topic).

Keep up with daily news, local and national. Regularly look over the magazines at the newsstand, check major news sources, and set up automatic Google searches for coverage of your topics. Check local and national TV and radio from time to time.

Also watch out for new movies and entertainment TV programs that might deal with your subject. Be prepared to comment on their coverage of the topic – or even use the new or upcoming movies/shows as launching pads for promoting your topic, book, or yourself.

Read the publications in your own field regularly. Know who the other experts are in your field, and who the opponents are.

If you want to be your own Publicist: Getting to the Press

First of all, it helps to do general research. Find out the breadth of the print and broadcast Media in your area. Make lists of potential Media markets (remember the online sources!) for your information and the specific people, publications and shows that might be appropriate to approach. Solicit friends and colleagues for contacts in the Media. When you make contact with media people, ask them for others contacts. In other words, do market research like you would for placing a written work or other product.

Network!

1) NEWSPAPERS/NEWS WEBSITES: Print and Online
    a. Find the appropriate place(s) for your story. Which paper? Which section of the paper?
    b. Who is/are the appropriate editor(s) or site managers?
    c. What are the story deadlines?
    d. Is it best to call or write first? For papers, write first. Use email when available
    e. Send a directed news release to the appropriate person(s)
    f. Cultivate contacts with news reporters/writers, columnists and bloggers. Keep feeding them info on a fairly regular basis once contact is established (as long as they show an interest)
    g. Don't badger
    h. Be careful of the use of "exclusives"
    i. Try to do your own calling/contacting. It's okay to have someone make the initial contact, or simply to send out press releases and inquiries, but be the one responding if you get a bite (unless you hire an actual publicist or PR person).

2) MAGAZINES: Print or Online
    a. Choose target publications carefully. The *WRITERS MARKET* book and website (www.writersmarket.com) and magazines like *Writer's Digest* can help in the background on the types of articles they buy, which tells you what to submit. Buy copies of the publication (most of them have digital formats to purchase as well as print) to get a feel for it.
    b. Who is/are the appropriate editor(s)?
    c. What are the story deadlines?
    d. Write a carefully constructed cover letter (as in a query letter). Use email when available.
    e. Send releases to all the appropriate editors, including the column editors and authors.
    f. You can often call an editor if you're pitching having the publication do a story *about* you/your subject, rather than one you're trying to sell.
    g. Cultivate contacts with staff writers, editors, columnists and free-lance writers.
    h. Don't badger
    i. Be careful of the use of "exclusives"
    j. Do your own calling/contacting. Don't leave it to a secretary.

3) WIRES
    a. News releases can be sent to the local wire bureau
    b. Always include a "Contact" phone number
    c. Consider *paid* wire services and paid press release distribution services.

4) TELEVISION AND RADIO
    a. Know the Shows. It's easy to say yes to everyone, but do a little research if possible and say yes to the appropriate ones, and especially to shows with large audiences or a big presence on the web. Be sure you'll feel comfortable with the host.
    b. Use email when available to contact them, but call rather than write when possible. *DO* send press releases and press kits in advance of calling, unless there's something too immediate about what you're promoting to allow mailing in advance.
        For TV shows: Check credits at the beginning and end of the shows for names of producers, associate and assistant producers, and "talent coordinators" or look to the show website. Don't try to contact the host directly.
        Individual reporters for TV news are good for contacts, but try to pick those who have done a decent job on similar stories in the past.
        For Radio: listen for the names of producers. If you can't get to the producer, you may contact the host (who often is the one booking guests for his/her own show). These days it's likely there's a webpage for the show. The programming director or news director of a station is often a good bet as well.
    c. Know Deadlines! Don't call the newsrooms or show line during the time immediately before or after a broadcast.
    d. Cultivate your contacts.
    e. Keep the story simple. On-air time is more an issue for TV than for Radio. If you're going for promotion of yourself as a talk show guest, *sell* yourself, but try not to spend too much time at it.
    f. TV needs visuals. Gather photos, videotapes, artist conception drawings or apparatus. If it's available, make it know to your contacts. If not, be prepared to brainstorm with the producer for possible visuals they might be able to gather.

5) THE INTERNET / WORLD WIDE WEB
    a. Research major sites on the web that deal with your subject
    b. Research the submission policies for online magazines / e-zines and who's running them
    c. Find podcasting and webcasting sites that interview guests in your field. Look for folks on YouTube with channels/web shows that interview people via Skype.
    d. Use *email* to contact them, unless the use of a phone and/or regular mail is indicated by the site

6) ALL MEDIA OUTLETS
    a. Learn as much as you can about their presence on the Web.
    b. If appropriate, use email to send materials to them. But do not SPAM multiple sites/media. Personalize the material.
    c. Do not send huge files unsolicited. A text email is more appropriate (with a link to a website), with a query as to whether the receiver would like to get more info.

Do It Yourself Media Training

There are several ways to prepare yourself for the Media in addition to the above. There are courses that can take you through training to be your best, books that teach you about public speaking and facing the media, and people like myself, who coach others and help with the ultimate goal of coming across well in front of a reporter, camera, microphone or audience. Many of us work both in person and via Skype with our clients.

You should learn the structure of the Media you seek to work with, so as to understand just how you need to present yourself and your information.

You should learn public speaking skills. Training in this area only makes you a better and more interesting interview subject and guest on TV or Radio shows – and will help you for speaking engagements about your book, your expertise and yourself as an author. This includes book signing events.

As far as the final skills in the interview are concerned, you can try a couple of exercises with friends or coworkers.

1. Use an audio recorder (you probably have a recording app on your smartphone) to stand in for the "radio" and conduct practice radio interviews. Designate a party as the "interviewer" and provide him/her with some information about what you'd like to discuss, and some sample questions.

Make sure he/she understands that you can be asked just about anything in the mock interview, rather than be limited to the provided questions.

There are excellent books out there on the art of interviewing that should help you.

Practice these interviews when possible in front of a small audience and ask for immediate feedback. You might also allow the audience members to play "call-in" with you and ask additional questions.

Replay the recording and discuss what the "show" (and you) sounds like. Repeat this with fresh angles (and perhaps fresh interviewers) until you feel comfortable with your performance.

Remember: you'll never be "perfect" in your own ears, so settle for comfortable.

2. Try the same thing with video. Set up a mock talk show setting and try the same as above, preferably with a small audience. Perhaps allow the audience to also ask questions, as with a real talk show.

Again, do the post-show critique.

Follow Up

One of the final points to keep in mind is that following up with the Media may help multiply future successes. Once you've worked well or even had a good contact with someone or some show, you should try not to lose contact. Every once in a while -- timing being a matter of intuition and reading the situation well; there's no set time for this -- re-establish contact with the people on the show or the reporter or whoever you had the most contact with (especially where it paid off in the past). Phone or email contact is generally best for this.

Realize that TV and radio shows (not so much podcasts) change personnel regularly. Getting the personal email of a contact means you can stay in touch even if he/she goes to another hopefully appropriate show.

Expertise and Credibility

As an "expert," you are expected to keep up on your topics. The Media people will often tell you to call them when something "new or exciting" happens in your arena, so they can be first to present it. Don't make a pest of yourself and continually call them; they will quickly tire of this. However, don't just sit back and expect them to call you (unless you can telepathically "nudge" them every now and then).

Keep on top of the local and national Media scene. When an event pops up, whether in the news or nonfiction literature, or in the movies or some other fictional media, jump on it. Contact your contacts and point out that you have something to say that would be of interest to their readers, viewers, listeners or audience and that it would enhance their presentation of the topic. In other words, appeal to their need to present the new and different (and perhaps the exclusive, where appropriate). If they notice the potential within that event, they might call you. Maybe.

Why wait? Act!

Also be prepared to be a resource for your contacts. If they most often call you for help with a story, whether it's information they need or a referral to another "expert," help them out without question or comment. I've found that this tactic has generated more media coverage for me than almost any other.

Finally...

The Media can be a wonderful force for promoting you and your writing, speaking or other "products." The very fact that you are interviewed or profiled in the paper, in a magazine, on TV or on Radio, gives you credibility and puts your name out in the public arena. In addition, this can prove to a potential publisher that you can do your own self-publicity -- this may be the edge that you need when trying to sell your next book or article. It can also prove or to an organization wanting to have you speak that you are recognized as an expert by others (not just by yourself).

All too often, lack of preparation and/or absolute terror of the Media has caused major downfalls in politics, business, the arts and science. You can stay on top of things with a bit of awareness of the methods of the Media and a willingness to make use of what the Media offers.

Remember to know your topic inside and out and to keep up with what else is going on in the Media related to your topic. In this way you can appear more the "expert" and avoid being confronted with dangerous surprises. Remember, too, that putting yourself out there as a *person*, someone very human, can make you more appreciated by the Media and called upon again and again.

ON THE USE OF SOCIAL MEDIA
FOR BOOK/AUTHOR PUBLICITY

And now to open that proverbial can of worms....

Working with Social Media can be a full time job if you let it (or if you can hired to do it). Many people, unless they're of shall we say more recent vintage don't even know where to start when it comes to promoting anything on Social Media. Even those who know something may not be keeping up with developments in the Social Media world, or even what's happening with websites and their migration to mobile platforms (smartphones, iPads and other tablets, Kindle and Nook tablets and mini-versions, etc) and apps for those platforms.

In the past, media presence has been a determining factor for a traditional publishing house to pick up an author-expert, and something that even aided fiction authors. These days, if you want to be traditionally published OR put it out there yourself, you are better off if you have a well-developed Social Media presence (hopefully in addition to some footprint in other media as well). In other words, you want to have an *author platform* already in place when your book launches.

WEBSITE...and GOING MOBILE

First, it goes without saying that you need a website. Think of it as your home base, from which you can launch any number of blogs, social media campaigns, sales for your books, info for the media (your extended bio and other materials that comprise a typical press kit), and updates on both upcoming and past media and speaking appearances.

These days, there is are a lot of individuals and companies that can build a website for you, and a wide range of pricing depending on how involved the build is and who you go to. Try finding someone local, which is easier than you think – there are all sorts of business networking groups (you can find them on *Meetup.com*) that typically include members who can do this for you, or others who can refer you to someone. You can also try one of the many folks (web designers) listed on *www.fiverr.com*, *www.guru.com*, or *www.odesk.com*.

Be sure to have a website designed that you can update yourself! A Wordpress-based site is pretty easy to update, add pages and posts to, and navigate. Naturally, you'll need a web hosting service for most of what they'll create for you. *GoDaddy.com*, where you can register domain names, also has hosting services.

Or if you have some creativity in you, and don't really want to pay anything for a site (or much at all, for simple add-ons), you can use *www.Weebly.com* or *www.Wix.com*, which offers free templates and hosting and are both incredibly easy to use to create and update websites. You can also go to *www.Wordpress.com* and use their free web design templates.

Be mobile-friendly! Do be sure your website looks good on smartphones and tablets. The statistics today show that more and more people are accessing websites from their mobile devices rather than desktop or laptop computers. If your site looks great on a computer, but lousy on a mobile device, your web traffic will suffer for it.

Have a really good bio of yourself on the site. If you're a fiction author, be sure to say something about why you decided to write, talk about your fiction, and mention how fans of your work can communicate with you. If you're a nonfiction author, do mention the book(s), but focus on the expertise behind the book(s), and how you not only can answer questions on the topic(s), but can also refer people to others in the same field.

Mobile app? Is there a way to adapt what you do and your books to a mobile application? More and more people are looking for simple apps to allow them to shop and interact. Think about how you might take content from your book(s) and your website and put it into a simple app that people can access from their smartphones and tablets. Again, check the above sites for "app developer." Wide range of people, and wide range of pricing. There are even companies that now offer template-driven apps for people to drop their information and activity into, which cuts the cost quite a bit.

SOCIAL NETWORKS

You probably already have a social network presence, such as an account with *Facebook, LinkedIn, Google+, Instagram, Pinterest* or one of the other similar-yet-different networks, but you may not know a few things to help you maximize promotion (of your work and yourself). If you do not have accounts (which are free) with the following, be sure to sign up for those that make sense to you. Below are a few tips for each of those services, but let me also mention that there are many other social networking services, and new ones popping up all the time, and some that are area-of-interest or organization specific.

Be sure to look for such interest/audience-specific social networks. Earlier in this book, Richard commented on *Goodreads.com* – which is a social network directed at book readers but also supports the efforts of authors promoting their books.

Also be sure to include links to all of your social media pages/channels with your signature on all your emails, as well as on your website. You can fairly easily add buttons to most websites that allow people to connect directly to those accounts/pages/channels.

If the network has special interest groups, be sure to find and join as many as makes sense to you (or as many as the service will allow; LinkedIn only lets you join 50). Besides posting promotional material or topical writing on the main pages of each of the networks, you can post in most of the groups you join – keeping in mind that some have specific rules as to what you can and cannot post that you should always review before posting anything.

Why join groups? Because many have hundreds if not thousands of "members" who might read and share your posts, thus expanding your reach that much more.

Facebook

Facebook has become the largest social network on the planet, currently with over one billion users. While originally designed as a *social* network (hence the reason you have "Friends"), it has increasing adapted to promoting/advertising products, services, and companies. While you may have a personal Facebook page, that merely scratches the surface of what can be done.

Your main page allows you to have "Friends." You can invite people, or say yes or no to people who invite you to connect. You have to decide what the main page is for – actual socializing/keeping up with real friends and acquaintances, promotion of your activities, or a little of both.

My own page on Facebook focuses on my paranormal-related activities (books, classes, events, media appearances). Consequently, I've approved request to "Friend" me by just about anyone and everyone. This has led me to hit the 5,000 "Friend" mark on Facebook (the limit of people I can have for the main page). I do occasionally look at the feed of posts from my "Friends," but with 5,000 of them, that could be a full time job in itself. So, when my actual friends (the ones I see and connect with more directly) post something, I rarely catch it. However, it's allowed me to reach a lot of people. [Note: Please do not try to "Friend" me on Facebook. I have the limit, and can't approve any more. *Do* go to my author page at *facebook.com/loyd.auerbach.author* and "*Like*" the page.

You may use that main page for promotion as I do of course, or shift all promotion to specific pages you can create for yourself as an Author or a page for each of your books or even a business you might have. It's easy to do so – from your home page, just look to the left column and you'll see a link to "Create Page." For author pages, they have an app that lets you easily fill in your bio and link to your books on Amazon.com. Whatever page(s) your using for promotion, be sure to post on all of them when posting on one.

Have a decent head shot or other shot of you as your profile picture, and yes, you can use it on all the other pages as well. There also should be some kind of relevant background picture you add at the top (think of this as the banner). Pictures increase page views.

Also, encourage people to go to your author page (or whatever pages you create) and click *Like.* This helps a lot with Facebook's search engine, and those folks are generally now following your activities (much like your "Friends" are with the main page). But the good news is that there is no upper limits for "Likes" on that page, which, if you're popular, can get you well past the 5,000 "Friend" limit.

Finally, as mentioned about, find and join groups on Facebook. Search on a term in the box at the top, then note there are categories that pop up across the new resulting page. Click "More" then click "Groups." Review and join the resulting groups, but do be somewhat selective. Go to each one and see a) how relevant the group's interests are to your book, your blog, your activities, you're your interests, b) how many people are in the group (the more the better, but some are just starting out and may be small to start), and c) if they're rules for posting are too restrictive (see the "Description" on the group page). Click "Join" for the ones you want to join – just know that many are closed groups where an administrator needs to approve you as a new member (based on your Facebook page).

When you post on your page(s), also post to all the groups you've joined, though know that some don't allow direct posting by members and your posts may undergo a review and approval/denial.

Be sure to ask "Please share" for all your posts, which can lead to more people re-posting to their own Friends and Followers.

Facebook also allows you to set up Events such as listing where you're speaking or doing a signing, or appearing on a podcast, radio or TV show. You can invite all your "Friends" or limit to more local groupings of them. You can also set up a book release party of sorts on Facebook, where you can calendar being available to respond to people's questions and comments live.

All in all, doing the above on Facebook allows your reach to extend to larger and larger groups of people.

LinkedIn

LinkedIn has typically been seen as a social network that skews much older than Facebook (and many of the others), mainly because it's set up to promote your work/employment and related business history. No question that it's business oriented, though that's been changing somewhat as groups are set up related to people's interests, not just what they're doing/have done for work. Younger people are also catching on to LinkedIn as a job search tool, so the demographics may indeed change.

"Connections" are what it's all about on LinkedIn (like "Friends"). What you post as your status on Facebook can also be posted on your LinkedIn account, and even (easily) reposted from there to Twitter.

Be sure to show yourself as an author in your profile, and to list your books. If you write a blog, be sure to use the "Post" feature on your LinkedIn home page and post there as well. If not, think about writing some articles you can post. The headline/title of the article should include keywords/terms that people might be searching for on Google, and do repeat the terms in the article where they make sense.

Also find and join LinkedIn discussion groups, and participate when/where appropriate – don't only post promotional stuff.

GoodReads.com

Beyond what Richard had to say, GoodReads has groups with varying interests, but be sure to focus on participation in discussions rather than shameless self-promotion. The former, especially when people know you are an author, counts for much more than simply talking up your own books. Certainly talk about the experience of writing, and the experience of being an author, but the GoodReads audience really appreciates participation as well as subtlety with promotion (and really does not like posting-for-promotion-only).

Claim your GoodReads author page, and make sure you fill out all your author details, then find and join groups.

Google+

Google+ --which is connected to any gmail account – is a social network that allows you to do much of the same posting as in LinkedIn and Facebook. It also allows you to connect with people and add them to "Circles" that you create. You can have specific groupings of your contacts, including separate ones related to your actual friends and family, to your personal interest, to your professional interests and expertise, and to your books. When you post, you can decide whether to make the post visible to the "Public,'" to specific circles or to all of them, and even to the extended circles of those in your circles.

Pinterest

Pinterest is more like scrapbooking and sharing articles, pictures, recipes, and other things you find that you "pin" to board. Authors can use this by finding really interesting stuff to pin and share. In other words, use it to show yourself as an *interesting person.*

When writing fiction, you can create boards that focus on the topics, places and kinds of people that are in your novels or stories. For nonfiction authors, focus on the topics of your expertise and book(s).

Instagram

Instagram is all about sharing photos and really short videos. Getting lots of pictures out there can certainly increase your presence in social media and, if you have pictures that become popular (and get transmitted to other social media such as Twitter), you can become a real online personality.

However, be sure to include the ever popular hashtag (#) with keywords so that when the appropriate keywords are searched, your photos will be part of the results.

MICRO-BLOGGING: saying things in few words

Twitter

People I've spoken with are often say they are afraid that once they get on Twitter, they'll have to be tweeting all sorts of things about what they're doing throughout the day, where they're going, etc.

Actually, Twitter has many kinds of tweets and users, including organizations, schools, companies, publishers, authors, and hiring mangers/recruiters, in addition to the celebrities, actors, music stars and others we hear about so often in the news.

Twitter allows for short bursts of information in 140 characters. Authors should tweet events and signings, links to blogs and articles they have written – or those they find interesting and think others may find interesting as well, something experts can do to further build up credibility and spread their expertise.

Tweet about your books, whether published or in process of being published. Tweet links to the books and ebooks on Amazon.com and to reviews of your books. You can shorten links at sites like *tinyurl.com, bitly.com, goo.gl,* and *ow.ly*

Tweets with pictures attached (of you, your book covers, interesting, yet relevant images) are more likely to be opened.

When people start to follow you, be sure to follow back the ones that make the most sense (especially those that have many followers themselves). Use the Retweet function to pass on tweets you happen to find that are of particular interest to you.

As for how often to tweet, it depends on how much you have going on or have to say. No need to post your meal choices, or day to day activity – keep it to what's connected to whatever it is you are trying to promote: your expertise (and topic of expertise), your books, your website, your blogs, your Facebook or LinkedIn longer posts, or yourself as a cool person, of course.

You can also share short videos on Twitter, but make them count! Make them interesting and relevant to your social media mission.

Oh, and be sure to list your Twitter handle as part of your signature, and ask that people follow you.

Tumblr is another micro-blogging platforms. On Tumblr you can share more than you can on Twitter, whether text, music, pictures, or videos and it provides ways to pretty up the post with colors and graphics.

BLOGGING

There are many platforms for blogging short or long articles and increasing your online presence, and of course you can do it on your own website. Write relevant pieces that support your general writing and publishing process and expertise. Fiction writers might blog a short story in several parts, or talk about getting background for characters and locations in their novels.

Blog about doing book signings and other events, especially if you have a really good question that might have come during the event. Do the same for responding to good questions that might come to you from email or other social media.

When you have a collection of blogs, remember that you can often bundle them together as an ebook (or even a print on demand volume).

In any event, blogs can be reposted on LinkedIn and Facebook, tweeted about, and discussed in other social media.

YOUTUBE

Like to video-record stuff? If it's something that your readers or audience would like, or that would draw people to you and your other social media (and your books, of course), upload it to YouTube! Create your own channel (easy to do) with your videos, and create Playlists of other videos of interest you find on YouTube. The more people connect with you and your interests, the more they'll find you and your books elsewhere.

One cool tool to create videos, even trailers for your books, is Powtoon (*www.powtoon.com*). It's an easy to use site that provides both a free and paid version to create animated videos to which you can add your own pictures/graphics (or use theirs), text, music (theirs or yours) or even do a voice-over. Very easy to use, and easy to "publish" to YouTube or other platforms.

AMAZON AUTHOR PAGE

Once you have books up on Amazon.com, be sure to claim and fill in your Amazon Author Page. It allows readers to see all your books in one place, read a bio, and even engage with you as an author.

EMAIL NEWSLETTERS

Writing a blog? Also send it out to people whose emails you gather. I suggest having a sign-up list for email at any presentations, lectures, book signings or other appearances.

Utilize email services like Constant Contact (*www.constantcontact.com*), Mailchimp (*www.mailchimp.com*), or Vertical Response (*www.verticalresponse.com*) to construct, schedule and send out newsletters. The services also provide a way to add a sign up auto-responder to your website – something very promotable on all the other social media. Let people know how to sign up and even post about what the newsletter might contain.

Send out a newsletter when you have content, but you might work to be on some kind of regular schedule. However, don't bury your contacts with too many newsletters and other emails.

EVENT PROMOTION SITES

You might also consider using event promotion sites like Eventbrite, Meetup.com and Zvents to invite people to your appearances and to find networking, writing, topic-of-expertise, or book-related events to go to in your local area.

SOCIAL MEDIA MANAGEMENT SITES/APPS

If you are able to plan out your posts, whether status updates, micro-blogs, or blogs/lengthier posts, you might want to consider using sites like *Hootsuite.com* or *SocialOomph.com.* These are but two of the services out there that provide a way for you to enter and schedule posts that will go across several platforms – which the site does for you.

Hootsuite allows you to manage up to three social media platforms for free, and has paid plans for more than that. *SocialOomph* also has a free plan, as well as paid services.

There are other similar services out there, with varying capabilities for free and lots more when you pay for them.

Twitter itself offers a free tool for tracking and organizing, as well as understanding and analyzing the engagement your tweets have out there. It's called *TweetDeck* (*www.tweetdeck.twitter.com*)

A QUICK SUMMING UP ON SOCIAL MEDIA

Simply, be present online.

Be relevant to your topic and/or your work in what you do and say.

Post across multiple platforms.

SOME PUBLICITY RESOURCES ON THE INTERNET

FOR AUTHORS AND SPEAKERS

Loyd Auerbach

These sites have free e-newsletters to sign up for!

http://www.bookmarket.com/
Book Marketing home page (John Kremer)

http://www.promotingyourbooks.com/index.htm
Promoting Your Books page

http://www.publicityhound.com/ The Publicity Hound

http://parapub.com/   Dan Poynter's Para Publishing web site

http://www.plannedtelevisionarts.com/ Planned Television Arts

http://www.rickfrishman.com/   Rick Frishman

http://www.anniejenningspr.com/publicitypro.htm
Annie Jennings PR

And another source for mailing lists and publicity:
http://www.bookannouncements.com/

Also visit the site for Writers' Digest at
http://www.writersdigest.com and the following sites for help for
new and unpublished authors. Some have free e-newsletters:
http://www.writersmarket.com
http://www.writermag.com/wrt/
http://www.author101.com/ (Note: Download a free directory of
writers' resources)
http://www.getpublished.com
http://www.writer-on-line.com/index.html
http://www.absolutewrite.com/

http://www.writingfordollars.com/
http://www.inktip.com/ (for screenwriters)
http://www.wga.org/ (Writers Guild of America)
http://www.creativescreenwriting.com/
http://www.speakernetnews.com
http://www.ecrossroads.com/epublishers.html (a directory of e-publishers and more)
http://www.jeffbelanger.com/blog/?p=42 (author Jeff Belanger's blog about writing & publishing)

A Few Internet-Based Publishers (besides CreateSpace & Nook)

http://www.iuniverse.com/
http://www.infinitypublishing.com/
http://www2.xlibris.com/
http://instantpublisher.com (Print on demand, self publishing)
http://www.lulu.com/ (Print on demand, self publishing)

KINDLE & NOOK MAKE IT EASY TO PUBLISH IN THEIR FORMATS!

Regarding Copyright Licenses:
http://creativecommons.org/

BOOK PROPOSALS:
THE OUTLINE FOR THE NON-FICTION BOOK

As mentioned earlier, putting together a non-fiction book proposal is not only important for selling a book to a mainstream publisher, but can be the skeleton on which you write (and finish writing) your actual book. Even if you are planning from the get-go to follow the self-publishing/print-on-demand process detailed here in this booklet, having the proposal will make your life and the writing process much much easier.

A couple of recommended books to help you with book proposals (I've used these in my Publishing & Media course as well as Richard Wren's earlier version of the booklet you hold in your hands):

Frishman, Rick and Robyn Freedman Spizman (2005). AUTHOR 101 BESTSELLING BOOK PROPOSALS: The Insider's Guide to Selling Your Work. Avon, MA: Adams Media.

Lyon, Elizabeth C (2002). NONFICTION BOOK PROPOSALS ANYBODY CAN WRITE: How to Get a Contract & Advance Before You Write Your Book. Perigee Books, updated edition.

Mettee, Stephen Blake (2012, 2nd ed.). THE FAST TRACK COURSE ON HOW TO WRITE A NONFICTION BOOK PROPOSAL. Quill Driver Books. [Note: this is one of the texts I've used for my *Publishing and Media* course at JFK University for years.]

Book Proposal Overview –
what should go into the proposal

IS THE IDEA SALABLE:

1. Who is the audience? Why would they want to read the book?
2. What else is available in book form at bookstores? Online booksellers?
3. Visit a good library...what's there? In the card catalog?
4. Books in Print ... what's in print/out of print?

5. Review competitive books that are currently in print
6. How is your book different? What does it add for the reader over the other books? Why might it be better (for the audience)?
7. Need to find at least one major difference, otherwise, possibly not salable.
8. Will your book – and its differences from the others – matter to the audience?

THE PROPOSAL:

1. It needs to be publishable (the proposal) – well written and professional

2. Include at least
   a. Cover letter
   b. Overview of the project, including:
      i. What's the book about
      ii. Generally, what's the structure/flow of the book
      iii. Who is the audience is, and who will buy the book
      iv. what are the competing books
      v. why this book is different (see above)
      vi. why people will care about the book
      vii. why you're writing the book (what interests you)
   c. Table of Contents
   d. Brief chapter descriptions
   e. Detailed outline/description of each chapter
   f. Author bio
   g. Promotion plans

3. You'll possibly need to include at least one chapter unless you're already published or have gained a name for yourself in the subject area of the book

4. Will the book have a forward, preface, introduction, afterword by someone else? If so, who?

5. Any appendices, resource guides, bibliography to be
    included?

6. If you're writing the intro, think about including that as a
    sample chapter (not really a necessity if you are going the self-
    publishing route)

7. If you have them, include endorsements of your
    work/expertise from others (authors or other experts),
    reviews of other work, samples of other published nonfiction
    (not really a necessity if you are going the self-publishing
    route)

Who is... Richard L. Wren started a new career writing novels at age 82, after retiring from a successful insurance career. His first novel, *CASEY'S SLIP*, took almost 3 years to finish and publish (2010). The book has had a screenplay adapted from it which is now in marketing.

Profiting from all the mistakes he made, he wrote and published his second book, *JOSHUA'S REVENGE*, in seven months. Now, at age 89, he published his third novel, *JUSTICE FOR JOSHUA*. Along the way, he wrote and published *A PRACTICAL GUIDE TO WRITING & PUBLISHING NOVEL*, an acclaimed, down to earth and fact specific "how to" booklet filled with the most practical advice for authors, which is being used as a text in writing and publishing courses. The book you hold in your hands is the newest version of that booklet, expanded and with an additional section on book promotion.

All of his books, and the forthcoming novel *Murder Made Legal: A Casey & Smitty Mystery*, have been published using the methods he is passing on in the book you hold. All are published under his Poor Richard Publishers company banner, and are available as both print and ebooks on Amazon.com.

Mr. Wren, a lifelong resident of Oakland, recently moved to Lafayette, CA, where he lives with his patient wife Betty.

Richard Wren is a fourth generation Californian. He has been the subject of TV pieces and newspaper articles as a great example of reinvention in retirement years. Richard L. Wren is a great example of someone who has reinvented himself and his career – especially so late in life. He's also a model for would-be novelists, both old and young.

  2014 for CASEY'S SLIP

Website: www.rlwren.com
Twitter: @WriteEZrightnow /
Facebook: www.facebook.com/poorrichardpublishers
YouTube: www.youtube.com/RichardLWren

Who is... LOYD AUERBACH, M.S. (Parapsychology), Director of the Office of Paranormal Investigations and President of the Forever Family Foundation, has been in the field for over 35 years focusing on education and field investigation. The author of 9 books including *The Ghost Detectives' Guide to Haunted San Francisco,* co-authored with the late renowned psychic Annette Martin. His latest release is *ESP WARS: East and West,* covering the psychic spying programs of the US and Soviet Union/Russia, co-authored by Dr. Edwin C. May (who ran the US program) and Dr. Victor Rubel, and available on Amazon.com and other online booksellers. He is a professor at Atlantic University and JFK University, and teaches Parapsychology (local and distance) through HCH Institute in Lafayette, California and online courses through the Rhine Education Center. He is on the Board of Directors of the Rhine Research Center and the advisory boards of the Windbridge Institute and the Forever Family Foundation. His media appearances on TV, radio and in print number in the thousands, including ESPN's SportsCenter, ABC's The View, Oprah, and Larry King Live. He works as a parapsychologist, professional mentalist/psychic entertainer, public speaking & media skills coach, and as a professional Chocolatier – and of course, an author (he's working on some new projects as he finishes this one).

Visit his public speaking site at *www.speakasyourself.com,* his chocolate site at *www.hauntedbychocolate.com,* and his main website at *www.mindreader.com*

Full bio: www.mindreader.com/info/loyd-auerbach/
Twitter: @profparanormal and @speakasyourself
YouTube: youtube.com/loydauerbach &
      youtube.com/profparanormal
Facebook author page: tinyurl.com/loyd-auerbachFBauthor
About.me: www.about.me/auerbachloyd
LinkedIn: www.linkedin.com/in/loydauerbach
Email: profparanormal@gmail.com or speakasyourself@gmail.com

CPSIA information can be obtained
at www.ICGtesting.com
Printed in the USA
FFOW04n2130231215
19964FF